Glow Guide™

Meditation

Glow Guide™
Meditation

**Simple Steps for
Health and Well-Being**

By *Andrea McCloud*

Illustrations by
Karen Greenberg

CHRONICLE BOOKS
SAN FRANCISCO

Library of Congress Cataloging-in-Publication Data:

McCloud, Andrea.

Meditation : simple steps for health and well-being /
by Andrea McCloud ; illustrations by Karen Greenberg.

    p. cm. — (Glow guide)
Includes bibliographical references.
ISBN 0-8118-3808-0
1. Meditation. I. Title. II. Series.
BL627 .M357 2003
158. 1'2—DC21
     2002014122

Manufactured in China

Designed by Greenberg Kingsley/NYC

Distributed in Canada by Raincoast Books
9050 Shaughnessy Street
Vancouver, British Columbia V6P 6E5

10 9 8 7 6 5 4 3 2

Chronicle Books LLC
85 Second Street
San Francisco, California 94105

www.chroniclebooks.com

Dedication
To Mom and Dad,
thank you for a lifetime
of support and love.

Mom, slow down.
Dad, stop worrying.

Acknowledgments
A big thanks to all of my friends
who claimed never to tire of hearing
about meditation. Special thanks to
Lynn for being a superior sounding
board, and to Derek for being an
ever-present source of love and
encouragement. Further thanks to
my editor, Mikyla, for being, well,
perfectly Mikyla, and to the team at
Chronicle Books for their hard work
and dedication.

Introduction

Glow is a state of being, a delicate blend of good mental and physical health, personal happiness, self-understanding, and self-confidence. You can't apply it, you can't wear it, and you can't special-order it; glow comes from within. It's an inner radiance that is realized by taking care of yourself and being good to yourself. It's you at your best.

At the core of your glow lies self-awareness. It is the foundation on which everything else depends. When you're comfortable with yourself, when you know yourself, when you accept yourself (your whole self, which means the good and the not so good), the other stuff—health, happiness, confidence—take root and begin to grow. The road to self-awareness can be bumpy, and it does take effort, but there is something that can help you along the way: meditation.

Meditating has been around for centuries, yet there is still a pervading haze of confusion over just what it means. It's actually pretty straightforward: *Meditation* is a fancy word for paying attention—paying attention to yourself and paying attention to your world. Any time you are focused on one thing or you are absorbed in a specific activity—be it painting or running or eating—you are meditating.

As simple as it sounds, for many of us it's not always easy. The mind likes to wander, and sometimes reining in our thoughts and blocking out noise and commotion is *tough.* Every day we're bombarded with myriad distractions that drain our energy and scatter our focus. Our packed schedules hold us captive, keeping us so wrapped up in the tedium of the day-to-day that we can't seem to stop—stop to see ourselves, stop to appreciate the world around us, stop to truly live. But there is a way to stop.

Enter meditation. Meditation brings us back to life. It wakes us up to ourselves and our surroundings. Through various tools and techniques, meditation teaches us how to slow down, clear our heads, and focus on the present. It helps us live in the moment, let go of outside distractions, let go of irrelevant thoughts and emotions, let go of attachments to the past, let go of anxiety over the future, let go of self-doubt and criticism, and get to know and come to value our world and ourselves as we are today, right now.

Meditation has many other subtle benefits. As we learn to focus and concentrate, miraculous things start to happen. We begin to think more clearly, observing thoughts and emotions with fresh eyes, free of assumptions and preconceptions. Our minds and bodies feel more centered and poised. We become more efficient in our activities. Stress, tension, and anxiety start to wither away, and we become more at home with ourselves and more comfortable in our own skin.

There's no right or wrong way to meditate, no rules or code of meditation. It is a very individual thing and takes many shapes and forms. All of the things you may associate with meditation—the breathing and sitting, the candles and chanting—are all simply techniques to help you on the road to meditation, but they are not meditation in and of themselves. The calm yet alert mind and body, the aware but relaxed state of being—now, that's meditating. And with some practice, the only tool you'll really need to meditate is your mind. It's true.

The thoughts and exercises in this book offer a simple guide to help you figure out what suits you and your lifestyle the best. All of the stuff that makes you uniquely you—likes, dislikes, work, family—will factor into what kind of meditation is right for you. It's really whatever you want it to be and whatever works for you. So keep that in mind while you're reading this book. Take some time with chapter 1, Traditional Meditations, and get acquainted with the idea and practice of meditating. Once you're comfortable with the basics, jump around the book. The exercises in the other sections range from active to artsy to freewheeling; experiment, see what feels good to you, and then stick with it.

And go easy on yourself. Focus and concentration take practice and patience. Don't give up and, most importantly, have fun!

Room to Breathe

It's safe to say that most of us don't pay much attention to our breathing or, for that matter, even take notice that we're breathing at all. We just do it, and like most good things, we take it for granted. But proper breathing is critical to our health and vitality, our mood and well-being.

Breathing not only supplies our cells with oxygen, it is what connects the mind and body. When your breath slows down, your body slows down. Simple as that. Think about it: When you're stressed and tense, undoubtedly your breaths are shallow and erratic, while when you're relaxed and peaceful, your breaths are most likely deeper and more even. The good news is we're in the breathing driver's seat—we have breath control. How we breathe is entirely up to us. We *can* breathe calmly, deeply, rhythmically, all the time; we just have to remember how.

Conscious breathing is a big part of meditation. It's pretty simple, awareness of the breath, but it takes thought and practice. The idea is to replace your small, quick, unconscious breaths with big, full, deliberate breaths—the kind that expand your abdomen and fill up your lungs from bottom to top. Spend a few minutes every morning getting in touch with your breathing. Before you get out of bed, lie on your back and put your hands on your abdomen. Inhale deeply; feel your lungs fill and your abdomen rise. Slowly exhale; feel your lungs empty and your abdomen fall. Do this several times. You can practice this mini meditation any time you need to reengage with your breathing—or yourself.

You can meditate anywhere, anytime, and in any fashion, but it's not always an effortless task (there are lots of distractions out there). Getting the hang of it will be easier in a calm and peaceful place. It will serve you well to set up a space in your home devoted specifically to meditation. Not only will this give you a tranquil place to meditate, but the space itself can be a source of encouragement and inspiration to keep you practicing. Here are a few simple tips on carving out your niche.

Creating Your Niche

* Pick a room or a secluded area in a room and claim it as your meditation space. You don't need anything too big, but it should be large enough that you feel comfortable and at ease in the space.

* Make sure the space is devoid of distractions. Look for a spot that is tucked away to avoid interruptions.

* The space should be clean and sparse. If it's full of clutter, spend some time tidying and cleaning. A messy room makes for an unsettled mind, so give your practice the advantage of a clean start.

* Equip the space with everything you'll need during meditation— a blanket, a timer, several pillows, a chair, a candle, a tape or CD player, anything particularly meaningful to you. You may even want to set up a personal altar (see page 29).

* Once you've carved out your space, spend some time there. How does it feel? Does it relax you? Do you need anything else, or is it just right? When you feel at ease and at home in your space, you're ready to begin.

Get Comfortable

Put on something cozy that suits the climate—nothing too tight or too loose. (Depending on your circumstances, you could also go in the buff! It's the closest we can come to our natural state, can be the ultimate in comfort, and is actually quite liberating! But you don't want to startle your roommate or the super, who "just came to fix the pipes," so use your discretion.)

Then spend a few moments stretching. Focus on your legs and back. It's easier to sit comfortably if your body is warmed up and loose.

Some of the seated postures require a level of flexibility that few of us can manage. Not to worry. Being limber is not a prerequisite for meditating. Sit in whatever fashion is most comfortable for you. Try the easy pose (cross-legged) or the kneeling pose. They are just as effective as the more advanced postures but demand less flexibility. And use a pillow if you need a little cushioning, or if sitting on the floor is just too hard on your body, grab a chair.

Have a seat, and get started!

CHAPTER ONE

Traditional Meditations

There are many different approaches to meditation, some unconventional, others more customary. Although they all serve the same purpose—to help you learn to focus—it's a good idea to experiment with the traditional meditations first. Once you understand just what it means to meditate and, more importantly, how your mind and body feel during meditation, it becomes much easier to carry your practice into other aspects of your life.

Sitting is the classic meditation position. Many people find it easier to focus if they're not moving. You don't *have* to sit to meditate; walking, standing, and lying down are also perfectly acceptable approaches to formal meditation and work well if you have a hard time sitting still.

During most formal meditations, you'll use a focal point. A focal point can be anything—an object or a sound, an idea or a smell, even your breath. It helps you clear away scattered thoughts, emotions, and general brain clutter by forcing you to focus your energies and attention on one thing. You'll learn more about this throughout the chapter.

In this chapter you will be introduced to all of the tried-and-true meditation techniques you'll need to initiate your practice. You'll find a wide range of exercises, from a simple seated meditation to the traditional Zen walking meditation, as well as a host of projects to help you create your own meditation tools. So flip to a page, and get your practice off to a good start by grounding yourself in the basics.

Jnana

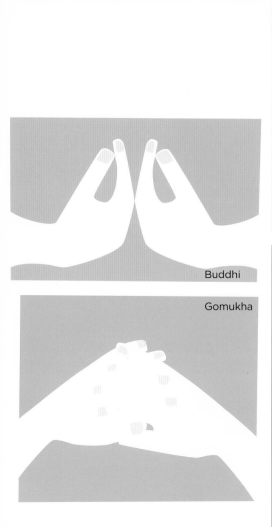

Buddhi

Gomukha

Atmanjali

When in a seated meditation, some people hold their hands in certain hand positions, or mudras. These sacred gestures redirect the energy released from the fingertips and return it to the body. How you position your hands during meditation is up to you. As always, make sure the hand position you choose is comfortable. And you don't have to stick with the same mudra each time you meditate. Pick the mudra that suits your mood from day to day. Here are a few to experiment with.

Mudra Madness

* **Buddhi:** Unifies all energies and puts them at peace. Use this one to calm down. Bring the tips of the thumb and index finger together. Relax your other fingers. Place the back of the hands together so the knuckles are touching, and rest your hands at the abdomen.

* **Gomukha:** Brings together the mind and the body, helping to focus energy. Interlock fingers, one thumb resting on top of the other. Place hands at the stomach.

* **Jnana:** Represents consciousness and is said to promote concentration. Place thumb and index fingertips together forming a teardrop, and relax your other fingers. Place your hands on your knees or thighs, fingers facing up.

* **Atmanjali:** Symbolizes gratitude and brings you inner harmony and balance. If you're feeling off center, try this one. Put palms together in prayer position and bring them to the heart.

Glow-How

If the mudras feel a little awkward, you can clasp your hands together and place them in your lap, or rest your relaxed hands on your thighs or knees. Resting the palms face up will open up your awareness and make you more receptive to surrounding energies, while placing your palms facedown will calm your mind and balance your personal energy.

A mantra is a sacred sound or a string of sounds that you can chant, sing, or speak aloud or in your head during meditation. The sound or vibration acts as your point of focus. There are many traditional mantras out there. Om, which represents the sound of the universe, is the most well known. You can use a familiar mantra or come up with your own. Any word or group of words that is meaningful to you can become your mantra; you just have to find something that feels right. Here's how to get started.

What's Your Mantra?

* Be on the lookout for words, phrases, and sounds that resonate with you. Flip through magazines and books of poetry, listen to song lyrics, and when something speaks to you, write it down.

* Once you've narrowed your mantra search to a few choices, give them a test run. Sing one, chant one, whisper one. How do you feel? Peaceful yet aware? Relaxed yet alert? Energized yet calm? If so, I'd say you've found your mantra.

* Now that you've found your mantra, try using it as your focal point during your next meditation. Just as you would focus on a candle flame or a small figurine, focus on the thought, sound, or vibration of your mantra.

Glow-How

Your mantra can act as far more than your point of focus. It is also there to give you strength and energy even when you're not formally meditating. If you're preparing for a big presentation, or maybe you just need a quick pick-me-up, take a minute with your mantra. Sing or say it a few times to yourself or aloud. How do you feel?

Thought so.

A mala *is a string of beads used in meditation for counting mantras or breaths (see Counting Your Breath, page 43). It is said to fill you with peace and bliss. A homemade* mala *can make a lovely gift for yourself or a friend and a nice addition to your meditation practice. The* mala *of a monk typically consists of 108 beads, but that's not necessary for your first* mala*. A wrist* mala *is the perfect size for beginners and will make for a unique beaded accessory!*

Blissful Beads

* String the twenty-seven small beads and then the large bead onto the nylon thread.

* Thread the loose end of the nylon cord through the large bead, forming a closed circle of beads, and knot the two ends together. Leave about two inches of thread hanging from the knot.

* Attach the premade tassel to the bracelet with the hanging thread, then snip off any excess thread.

What You'll Need

Twenty-seven 8mm beads

One 12mm bead

Two yards of nylon thread with fixed needle

Premade tassel

Scissors

Glow-How

Hold your *mala* loosely in your hand. (Traditionally it's held in the right hand, but hold it in whichever hand is more comfortable.) Move the *mala* bead by bead between the thumb and middle finger as you repeat your mantra. Remember to pause between recitations. The moment of silence between each mantra is also an important part of your practice. Once you've circled the strand and have reached the *meru* (the large bead), which represents wisdom, begin again, this time moving in the opposite direction.

Mandalas are circular designs used as focal points. Typically composed of concentric circles, they are meant to symbolize the journey of self-realization and the path to one's center. You "enter" into the mandala, and as you move toward its center, you move toward your center. You can find mandalas in books and magazines, or you can get creative and make your own. Making your own mandala can be a powerful form of meditation in itself. It's a cathartic way to spend an afternoon or quiet evening getting to know yourself and discovering all of the miraculous qualities that make you you.

Custom-Made Mandala

Here are instructions for making a basic outline for your mandala; the rest is up to you. Mandalas can be quite simple or exceptionally elaborate, so use any colors, patterns, pictures, or little extras that catch your eye.

* The circle is a primary component of a mandala, so start there. Put the bowl facedown in the center of the paper. Using a marker or pencil, trace around the perimeter of the bowl, creating a perfect circle.

* Put the quarter in the center of your circle. Hold it steady and trace its perimeter.

* That's it! Now you're ready to add the details. Remember, mandalas represent the layers of our being, so include colors, images, words, and symbols that are meaningful to you and will help you on your journey toward self-discovery.

What You'll Need

Medium-sized bowl

Blank paper

Markers or colored pencils

A quarter

Glue (optional)

Photographs (optional)

Cutouts from magazines or newspapers (optional)

Your personal altar is a special spot where you can display the little things that are particularly meaningful to you and to your meditation practice. It creates an intimate backdrop for meditating and also serves as a constant source of inspiration. Like a traditional altar, it's a sacred space for worship and a place of peace, but here, the religion is you.

Altar of Awareness

* Find a spot in your home that is quiet, comfortable, and uncluttered.

* You'll need to set up a small table or bench. If neither are available, clear out a single bookshelf.

* Unearth your favorite things: special mementos, candles, paintings, postcards, letters, photographs, seashells, books, plants.

* Place all of your special items on the table. Organize them in whatever fashion suits you.

* Use your altar as a point of focus, as a home for your meditation tools, or as a private place to be with yourself.

Glow-How

For a little bit of peace and calm to go, take a small item from your altar and carry it with you. Perhaps keep that special quote tucked in your wallet, or carry the seashell in your pocket. That way, you'll always have a special place to meditate, no matter where you go.

Performing an opening ritual before you meditate, much like the bows used in zazen, *is a great way to initiate your meditation session. It calms your mind and brings you into the present moment. Each time you perform your ritual, you are telling your mind and body, "Right now, I'm beginning my meditation." There are many traditional approaches, but really your ritual can be anything you want it to be. Recite a poem, sing your mantra, reach your arms to the sky—all of these can be opening rituals. Do whatever feels good and natural to you.*

Openers

* Take a few moments before your next meditation session and create a ritual. Experiment. Do you like sound? Try a bell or a clap. What about smell? Light some incense or a fragrant candle.

* The ritual should be simple. You want it to become a habit, an ongoing part of your practice. The easier it is to do, the more apt you are to do it with regularity.

* Once you've established your ritual, do it before each meditation session. Routine is an important part of your practice, so stick with one ritual. Soon it will become part of your practice, and each time you perform your ritual you'll put yourself into a meditative state of mind.

Zazen is the Zen Buddhist term used to describe seated meditation. It is a little different from the other forms in that you don't focus on one particular thing. The idea is actually not to concentrate but to observe. You are "just sitting" in a constant state of awareness.

Here are the particulars associated with zazen. *You may want to become familiar with them, especially should you choose to attend a formal sitting in a* zendo *(Zen meditation hall). Some people enjoy the rituals and structure, but others do not. As always, how you meditate is your choice;* zazen *is just one of many different approaches.*

The Zen Way

* Place your hands in prayer position, or *gassho*. By putting your hands together, you are bringing both sides of yourself together.

* Bow to your seat and then to your altar. In doing so, you are recognizing the wisdom in yourself and the wisdom in those who came before you.

* To achieve better balance and stability, *zazen* uses a three-point seated position. Sit down on your *zafu* (small pillow) and *zabuton* (flat cushion or mat) either cross-legged or kneeling pose.

* Use the *zafu* to get into a comfortable position. Sit on it, put it between your ankles, whatever feels good. You may even need two. You should be tilted forward slightly so that your knees rest on the *zabuton*.

* Set your timer for five to ten minutes. (No, Zen Buddhists don't use timers, they ring bells, but your timer is a viable home substitute.)

continued >

* Rock side to side and forward and backward until you find the spot where you feel completely centered and stable. Lift your chest, straighten your spine, and relax your shoulders.

* Rest your left hand in your right hand, fingers facing each other, palms up, the tips of your thumbs touching. Bring your hands to your stomach, about an inch below your belly button.

* Fix your eyes on a point a few feet in front of you. Don't focus; use a soft, open gaze.

* *Zazen* is about observation, not one-pointed focus, so as you settle into your meditation, observe how your body feels and what emotions and thoughts surface. Don't concentrate on any specific thought or feeling; simply watch them come and watch them go.

Music can serve as a great focal point for meditation. As its soothing sounds relax and calm you, the steady beats and even rhythms help capture your attention and maintain your concentration. Pick a favorite CD—something mellow, nothing too distracting—and take a seat.

Meditating to Music

* Turn on the music.

* Sit cross-legged on the floor. Make sure you're sitting up straight and your shoulders are relaxed. It may be a bit more comfortable if you sit on a pillow.

* Set your timer for five minutes. (When you're just learning to meditate, it helps to use a timer. This automatically eliminates two huge distractions—clocks and watches.)

* Place your palms on your knees and slowly rock side to side, forward and backward, until you find your center and feel balanced and stable.

* Rest your eyes comfortably on a spot in front of you. Keep your mouth relaxed and closed, and breathe through your nose.

continued >

Glow-How

There are CDs composed specifically for meditation. Check your local record store—there's usually a special section devoted to music for relaxation. If it comes up dry, most slow and mellow music will also do the trick.

Glow-How

Sit cross-legged or in the kneeling pose whenever you get a chance—watching TV, talking on the phone, reading, or hanging out with friends. This will help your body get more and more familiar with the position and will gradually make the posture more comfortable and easier to maintain during meditation. If you've got bad knees, stick with a chair.

* Focus your attention on the music. Let thoughts and emotions drop away as your mind follows the rhythms and the beats. Your mind and body should be quiet and steady, relaxed yet alert.

* Your mind may start to wander off; don't panic—it's okay. Acknowledge the thought and then let it go. The idea behind meditation is not to cease all thoughts and emotions—that's pretty much impossible. The goal is to let them come and go without latching on to them, to be aware but unattached.

* When the timer goes off, take a moment to thank yourself for participating, and slowly get up.

Some people find kinhin, *the Zen Buddhist version of walking meditation, to be a bit tedious—the pace is exceedingly slow. But others find it a nice break tucked in between seated meditations. Regardless of which school you may think you fall into, it's definitely something to try at least once.*

Take It Slow

* Make sure you've got space to walk, about ten to fifteen square feet.

* Set your timer for five minutes.

* Hold your upper body as if you were in a seated meditation: back and neck straight, shoulders relaxed.

* Make a fist with your right hand, thumb inside, and cover it with your left. Bring your hands to your stomach keeping elbows out from the body.

* Walking in a clockwise circle, inhale as you slowly lift your right foot. Continue inhaling as you bring the right foot forward.

* Exhale as you place the foot, heel then toe, down about three to six inches in front of the planted foot. Be aware of your foot as it touches the ground and the forward shift in your body weight as you step. Your movements should be slow and deliberate—you are taking one step for each complete breath (an inhalation and an exhalation).

* Begin the cycle again with the left foot.

* Remain completely aware and present in your movements.

Meditating at the end of a grueling day is a good way to let go of lingering tension and anxiety before hitting the sheets. Not only will it clear your head for the next day, it will help prep your body for sleep. Tonight, instead of flipping on the television to unwind, light a candle and try the kneeling pose.

Nighttime Nirvana

* Light a candle and set it a few feet in front of you, close enough that you can see it comfortably but not so close that it becomes intrusive.

* Place a small pillow vertically between your ankles, under your buttocks. Keep your knees together and sit back on your heels. Do you feel supported? If not, you may need a firmer pillow.

* Shift your body around until you are centered and comfortable.

* Set your timer for five minutes.

* With your spine straight and your shoulders relaxed, place your palms on your knees or in your preferred mudra (see Mudra Madness, page 21).

* Keep your mouth closed and breathe through your nose.

* Concentrate on the flame. Focus on its colors and movements, the subtle way it changes shape. Slowly all outside distractions should start to fall away. With some practice, your concentration will be effortless and free-flowing.

* When the timer rings, thank yourself for showing up to this meditation session and for taking time out for yourself, and leisurely get up.

Glow-How

Try not to think about the fact that you're meditating—just meditate. Don't force yourself to feel any particular way; let your body and mind get comfortable and move at their own pace.

Feeling off-kilter or need to focus? Turn to your breath; it has an amazing calming effect. By bringing you into the present and putting you back in touch with your mind and body, conscious breathing helps you regain balance and composure. Breath counting is a quick and easy way to engage with your breath any time you need to come back to yourself.

Counting Your Breath

* Sit anywhere and in whatever fashion suits the circumstances. Get comfortable.

* Breathe naturally. Listen to the sound of your breathing. Relax.

* Start counting your breaths (an inhalation and an exhalation equal one breath). If you've made a *mala,* use it to help you keep track of each breath.

* Once you reach ten, you can stop or begin again at one.

Glow-How
***

A bonus to using your breath as a focal point is that it's always with you, any time, anywhere. So whenever and wherever the mood to meditate strikes you, all you need to do is take a breath and begin.

Meditating on the floor isn't necessarily the right approach for all occasions and circumstances. If you're at work or hanging out in a café, using a chair is obviously more sensible. And for some people, it's just more comfortable. Dhyana (Sanskrit for "meditation") can be done sitting anywhere, so take a seat at home, at work, or even on the bus, and get started.

Dhyana at Your Desk

* Sit in the chair with your back straight. Keep the chest lifted and your shoulders relaxed. Make sure you are centered and comfortable.

* Set your timer for five minutes.

* Plant your feet on the floor, relax your legs, and rest your palms on your knees or thighs.

* Breathe. Follow the natural rhythm of your breath as you inhale and exhale. What does it feel like coming in and out of your nose? How do your lungs feel as they begin to fill? Feel your abdomen rise and fall. Try not to attach any feelings to your breath; just "watch" it.

Shavasana, or corpse pose, is a yoga posture that also serves as an especially effective meditation technique. Like the other traditional methods, it helps your body relax so that your mind can focus. But unlike the others, it allows your entire body—every organ, bone, muscle, joint, and tendon—to relax, which helps you to move even deeper into your meditation. It seems pretty simple, but actually it can be a little tricky. Shavasana is not meant to be a precursor to a nap; the key is to remain awake and alert, yet fully relaxed.

Play Dead

* Set your timer for ten minutes.

* Lie on your back. Make sure you're lying on something comfortable, like carpet or a thick blanket. But don't get too cozy—no drifting off!

* Your legs should be slightly separated and straight but relaxed. Let your feet fall outward.

* Rest your arms slightly out from your sides, palms up.

* Follow your breath until it becomes rhythmic and smooth. Then turn your attention to relaxing your body.

* Starting at your feet, feel the calm run up your legs; into your abdomen; course through your spine, chest, and arms; and finally inch its way into your neck and face.

* When you're completely relaxed, go back to your breath. Breathe in and out, slowly, peacefully, evenly. Let your mind follow your breath. Feel your body fall away.

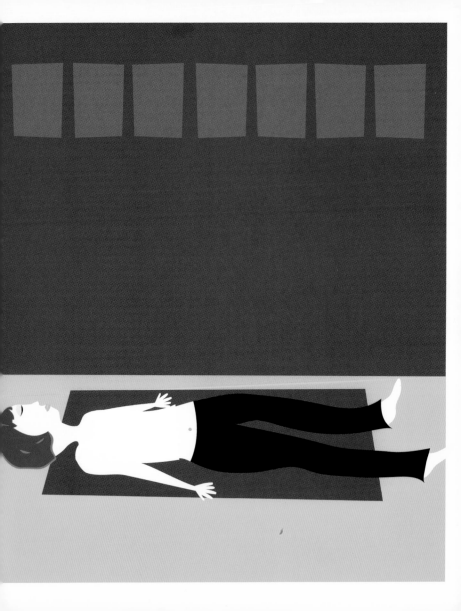

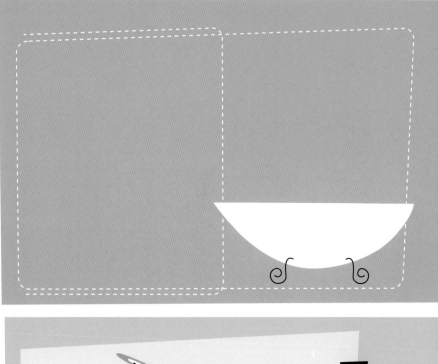

Add a lavender-and-flaxseed eye pillow to your shavasana *practice and see what it really means to relax. The pillow can also be used to soothe headaches, eyestrain, and tense facial muscles. The lavender is calming and restorative, and the flaxseeds mold to your face and temples, helping to achieve the same tension-relieving effects as acupressure. Here's how to make one of your very own.*

Rest Your Eyes

What You'll Need

¾ cup flaxseeds

1 cup
dried lavender

Small bottle
of lavender oil

Bowl

One 16-by-5-inch
piece of fabric
(something soft
to the touch,
like silk, satin,
or velvet)

Needle and thread

Scissors

* Mix the flaxseeds, dried lavender, and three drops of essential lavender oil into a bowl. Let sit.

* Fold the fabric in half, the plush sides of the fabric on the inside, creating an eight-by-five-inch rectangle.

* Stitch along the sides of the rectangle, leaving two inches at the top unstitched. You don't want any of the seeds or lavender slipping out the sides of the pillow, so make sure they are securely sewn. You may even want to do another round of stitching.

* Turn the pillow right-side out.

* Slowly pour the flaxseed-and-lavender mixture into the pillow.

* Stitch up the remaining two inches of fabric. Then put your feet up, rest your pillow over your eyes, and relax.

Glow-How

Cool your pillow to relieve puffy, swollen eyes, and heat it up to help with sinus congestion.

CHAPTER TWO

Moving Meditations

There are many ways to meditate. While sitting is a common practice and works really well for a lot of people, in truth, it's not going to work for everyone. Movement meditation offers another path to a meditative mind that may be more in sync with your step. The same principles are applied—mindfulness, awareness of yourself, awareness of your breath—just packed up and taken on the road.

Walk, dance, run, bike—whatever your urge or inclination, the seven exercises that follow will show you the art of meditation on the move.

A meditative walk gives you the opportunity to experience not only yourself but your environment. And you don't have to hit the hiking trails or head out to a nature reserve to do it (though that's nice, too); a simple spin around the block is a great way to do a little universal exploration. Be aware of yourself and in tune with your surroundings. Don't think about the past or the future. Right now, you're just walking.

Sidewalk Stroll

* Put on some comfortable shoes and head outside.

* First, banish the thought of destination. Walking meditation isn't about where you're going; it's about how you got there, and living absolutely in the moment, footstep to footstep, breath to breath.

* Walk a little bit slower than you normally do. Remember, you're not racing to get somewhere.

* Breathe naturally.

* Consider how your body is feeling. Are your muscles loose or tight? Do your feet feel light or heavy? What's your mood? Don't judge, just observe.

* Eventually turn your focus to the external. Allow yourself to become totally absorbed in the environment. Engage all of your senses.

* What colors do you see? What sounds do you hear? Take a deep breath. Can you place a particular smell?

* Stop for a moment and touch a lamppost, a flower, or a leaf. What's the texture?

* Continue walking mindfully for thirty minutes.

Glow-How

The next time you have to pick up milk at the corner store or you want to rent a movie from that place down the street, trade in the car keys for a pair of comfortable shoes and walk. Walking is an easy way to incorporate meditation and some valuable quiet time into your busy schedule. And the extra exercise doesn't hurt either.

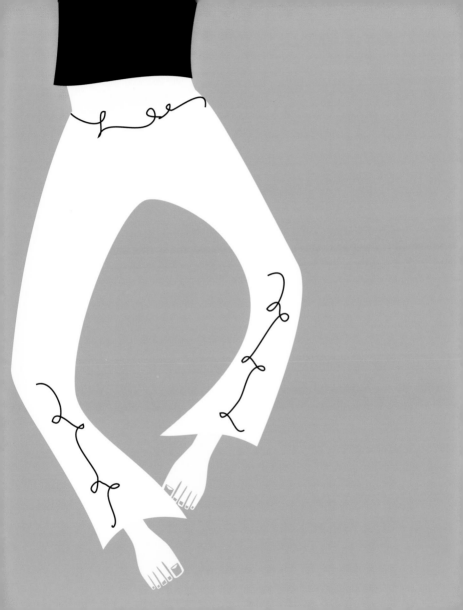

*Shaking your booty can be its own form of meditation,
or it can serve as a precursor to seated meditation.
Dancing helps ready the body for sitting by liberating any
pent-up energy, emotions, stress, or anxiety that you've
stowed away throughout the day. Oh, and it's a lot of fun!*

Get into the Groove

* Set your timer for fifteen minutes.

* Take off your shoes and turn on some of your favorite dance tunes.

* Take a deep breath, and let loose! Move your body around, pump your arms, swing your hips, spin wildly, jump, kick, karate chop, fandango like never before. Don't worry about how good your moves are—just have a good time.

* Try to breathe normally. No need to pay any special attention to your breath; your only focus should be getting your groove on.

* When the timer rings or you're sufficiently winded, click off the music and sit or lie down.

* Be silent and still. Feel your entire body relax and your heartbeat begin to slow. Spend the next five to ten minutes being aware of your body and your breath.

Yoga and meditation are very close allies. Sometimes yoga is used as a prelude to meditation, and sometimes yoga is the meditation. In both practices, the goals are the same: self-awareness, mindfulness, and focus. However, their approaches can be a little different. Where the traditional seated postures use stillness as a means to the meditative mind, yoga incorporates bodily movement, balance, strength, and stamina.

The tree pose is a basic standing asana *(posture) that helps develop balance and concentration. Learning how to balance the body helps you learn how to balance the mind. Spend a few moments in the tree pose when you need some help finding your center.*

The Asana Alternative

* Stand upright with your feet slightly apart and your hands at your sides.

* Transfer your weight onto your right leg. Engage your thigh muscles. Bend your left leg and place the sole of your left foot against the inside of your right thigh. Make sure your hips remain even.

* Bring your palms together in front of your chest and slowly lift them over your head until your elbows are straight.

* Let go of any tension and settle into the posture. You should feel strong but not rigid.

* Keep your chin level and focus on a point directly in front of you. This will help you maintain your balance. Breathe slowly and consciously. Focus on how your body feels in the posture. Hold the position for ten seconds. Then slowly release and switch sides.

Glow-How

For more information on yoga, check out *Glow Guide: Yoga.*

Spending time outside, regardless of where you are, is a treat to yourself and to your soul. But if you're lucky enough to live near the country, the mountains, or even a neighborhood park, the trees, flowers, and foliage make a great outdoor sanctuary for walking meditation.

One with Nature

* Put on some comfortable clothes and your walking shoes and head to your favorite hiking trail.

* Once you've started your trek, begin focusing on your movement and how your body feels. Walk slowly! Be aware of each step. What does the ground feel like underneath your feet? Is the air cool against your face? Really observe how your body moves and responds to nature.

* Turn your attention to your breath. How has it responded to the environment? Is it slow and steady or has it quickened up a bit? Follow the fresh air as it enters your body and fills your lungs.

* Now try to walk in sync with your breath. Take four steps as you breathe in and four steps as you breathe out. (Or do whatever feels comfortable and natural. If you prefer taking three steps for every inhalation and five steps for every exhalation, that's fine. Just be consistent and find a rhythm.)

* Notice what's going on around you. Really see the trees and flowers. Put yourself fully in nature. No thoughts of work or errands, the past or the future. It's just you and the oak trees.

* Feel your stress and worries float away as you discover a new appreciation for yourself and your surroundings.

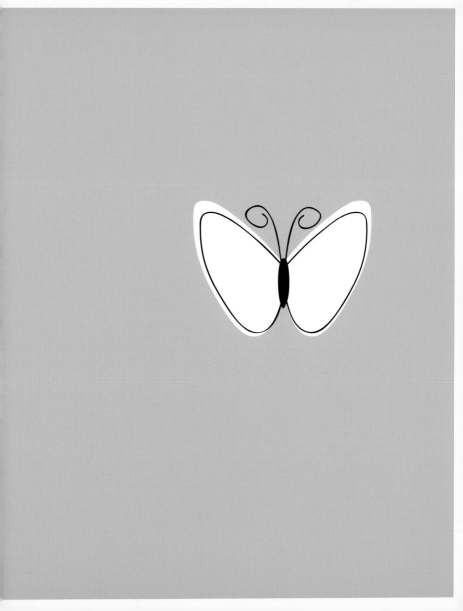

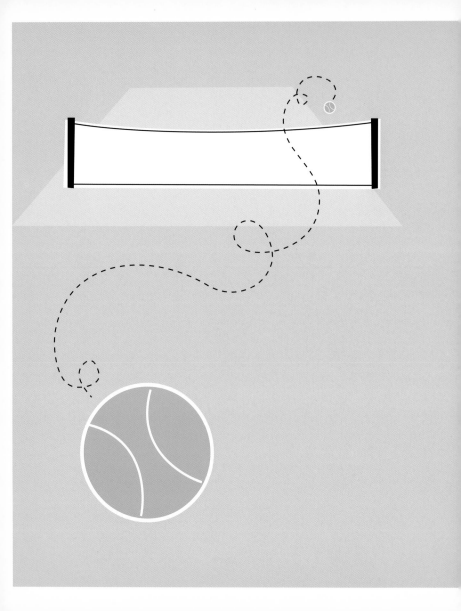

Meditation can be summed up in one word: flow. Remember the tennis match, bike ride, or afternoon jog when you were so completely and utterly absorbed in the action that you lost track of time, shut out all noises and discomforts, and were one with your racket, bike, or sneakers? That's flow.

Learning to find your flow during your favorite sport will eventually help you harness the essence of flow in the other, more mundane of life's activities—doing the dishes, walking the dog, even cleaning your closet.

Be the Ball

* Pick your favorite physical activity. Prepare as you normally would and head outside.

* Give yourself a few minutes to warm up and then slowly start clearing your mind of anything other than the act of running, riding, or whatever it is you're doing.

* Once you've taken a few moments to shake off any extraneous thoughts and have worked out any tight muscles, turn your concentration up a notch, and start to focus entirely on the activity at hand.

* Distractions and time should slowly begin to fall away.

* If your mind starts to stray, that's fine; follow your thoughts and slowly bring them back to what you're doing.

* In the beginning, shoot for ten-minute intervals of active meditation. Before you know it, an hour will have flown by.

Sesshins are intense weeklong Zen meditation retreats where you spend most of the day—starting as early as 4:30 A.M. and running as late as 10:00 P.M.—either in meditation or studying meditation. Your own sesshin need not be so ambitious; a single Saturday can serve the same purpose: personal enlightenment! Here are some not-so-traditional ideas on how to reach nirvana.

Create a schedule that suits you. Here is an example.

Saturday Sesshin

What You'll Need

Thick blanket

Plump pillow

Hard-boiled eggs

Fresh fruit

Journal and pen

Good tunes

Household cleaning supplies

Salad fixings

Sneakers

Candles

Bubble bath

Cleansing face mask

Pizza delivery number

Movie rental

Chamomile tea

* Start your morning with a fifteen-minute seated meditation. This may be a little longer than you're used to, but give it a try. Use the blanket and pillow to ensure complete comfort.

* Have a breakfast of two hard-boiled eggs and fresh fruit. The perfect morning meal, it doesn't weigh you down and it gives you energy for the day to come.

* Spend thirty minutes writing in your journal. Let go of pent-up thoughts and emotions. Write down whatever comes to mind.

* Now on to the dirty work. Turn on some tunes, roll up your sleeves, and pull out the elbow grease— it's time to clean. First spend some time purging. Your pantry, closet, and medicine cabinet could probably all use a good once-over. Letting go of "stuff" and clearing away clutter in your home can help you clean up your emotional space, too.

continued >

* Eat a light lunch. Design your own *sesshin* salad, packed with vitamins and minerals and tons of flavor. Throw on some walnuts, blue cheese, cranberries, or apples—whatever tempts your taste buds.

* Put on your sneakers and go for a long walk. Walk slowly and observantly, of course. Watch the sunset.

* Light a candle, fill the bathtub, apply your face mask, and soak for one hour.

* Call the pizza guy and order dinner. Throw in the movie, wrap yourself in a blanket, settle in, and enjoy.

* Fix yourself a cup of calming chamomile tea and prepare for slumber. Hit the sheets relaxed and renewed, and wake up on Sunday feeling like a new person.

Meditating in foreign surroundings is a great way to learn something new about yourself and your world. A white-sand beach, a nineteenth-century cathedral, and a café next to the Seine are all wonderful places to meditate. And remember, your meditation isn't limited to particular locations; your journey from place to place is yet another opportunity to fine-tune your awareness and wake up your soul.

For the Traveler

* Practice a walking meditation in London's Trafalgar Square.

* Ride a bike around the Latin Quarter of Paris.

* Do a breathing exercise on the train from Boston to New York.

* Mindfully ascend to the top of the Duomo in Florence.

Glow-How

If you're traveling abroad, take precautions. Do your research and know what's going on politically in the country before you get there. Once you arrive, be careful. Don't carry a lot of money or valuables with you, and do be aware of your surroundings. It's also a good idea to have the number and address of the American embassy jotted down somewhere, just in case.

CHAPTER THREE

Creative Meditations

Creating anything is invigorating and cathartic. Your art, whatever form it may take, is yet another vehicle through which to channel your energy and focus, release pent-up thoughts and emotions, and discover something new about yourself. Don't let the word *art* scare you. Creative meditation is about one thing and one thing only—expressing yourself. All you need is an open heart and mind, and a playful imagination.

In this chapter, you'll get the chance to do lots of artsy stuff, like write a haiku, try your hand at a Japanese ink painting, sing your heart out, and tend a rock garden. Don't be intimidated by any of the exercises; talent is absolutely unnecessary. Ditch your inner critic (see page 75 to learn how), let your creative juices flow, and have some fun.

Keeping a journal is a very powerful meditation tool. It works on multiple levels. It can be a receptacle for the mental garbage that's blocking your concentration or creativity. It can be a road to self-discovery, as you peel off the layers of yourself with each page. It can be a place to record the details of your day, your sentiments from a mindful walk, your observations from the bus ride home. The form of your journal will most likely evolve as you do, but its purpose will remain the same: to give you a private place to let it all out.

Write It Down

* Buy yourself a nice journal, something sturdy but small enough so you can carry it around in a purse or bag if you feel so compelled.

* Start writing in your journal every day. Say anything. This is your time to let everything go.

* Try writing for at least five minutes without putting your pen down.

* Write down every thought, idea, impulse, sensation that comes to mind as it comes to mind. Your tooth hurts. You love your job. You like the feel of your blouse on your skin. You want to go to Paris and learn French. Shoot, you forgot your keys, no, you've got them. You're hungry. The woman next to you is reading your favorite book. The bus smells. Get the idea? Include every detail— write them all down!

* Don't worry about your "writing." Journal writing doesn't require proper grammar or even punctuation. This is not for anyone else to read. It's all yours. Simply put pen to paper, move your hand across the page, and see what surfaces.

Drawing meditation is an exercise in self-expression and observation. Think of it simply as a journal translated into pictures, a visual record of thoughts, feelings, impressions, and self-discovery. Don't worry about your artistic skill (or lack thereof); it doesn't matter. Your drawings are not for public consumption. This exercise is about connecting with your subject and yourself.

Visual Journal

* You'll need a sketchbook, a pencil, and about fifteen to thirty minutes.

* You can draw anywhere—in your house, in the park, in a café. Just make sure you can sit comfortably for up to thirty minutes.

* Pick a subject, any subject—a teacup, a leaf, a flower, another person, your hand—and start drawing. Draw whatever you see. Don't be concerned about the quality of the drawing; it's not the image that matters, it's the action! Let your pencil move freely—you can't make a mistake. . . No, you really can't! Just draw.

* Feel time, distractions, thoughts, and emotions fall away as you, your pencil, and your subject unite.

As we race here, dart there, it is easy to become complacent in the way we see our world. We accept and assign names, expectations, and judgments to objects, places, even people before we've fully experienced them for ourselves. The solution: a simple shift in perspective.

The Flip Side

* Grab a pencil, your sketchbook, and an everyday object—a jar, stapler, tape dispenser.

* Set the object upside down on your desk or table. (This will help you lose whatever attachments you might have to the object's intended use.)

* Disregarding anything you know or think you know about this object, look at it simply as a form. Notice its shape, colors, patterns, and any other details or subtleties.

* Begin to draw the object as you see it today, in this moment, from this perspective. Let go of any former thoughts or opinions you held about the object and draw it as it exists before your eyes right now. Don't be startled if the object transforms into something entirely new to you, maybe even something beautiful. That's your Zen vision at work.

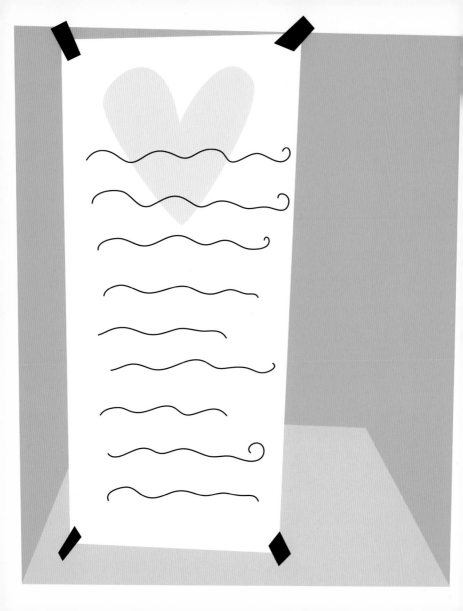

If you're like most people, you can probably find countless ways to criticize and belittle yourself, especially when your creativity and artistic skills are the subject, but you get tongue-tied when it comes to articulating anything positive or self-affirming. This is not really your doing; it's the work of your inner critic. Your inner critic never has anything nice to say and is full of faulty opinions and misguided theories. Here's how to boot that little bugger out of your life for good.

Banish Your Inner Critic

* Grab some paper and a pen.

* Make a list of all of the things you absolutely hate about yourself. Whatever comes to mind, write it down.

* Set it aside for a moment.

* Now, in the same fashion, make a list of all of the things that you love about yourself. Again, jot down everything that comes to mind. Dig deep; have the courage to really see yourself. Make this list longer than the first—do not stop until it is! Your voice, your curly locks, the way you help others, your wit, your intelligence. Include it all without criticism or qualification.

* Once you've identified your stellar qualities and committed them to paper, place your list in a very prominent spot in your room. (Or you may want to carry it in your wallet.) Make sure it's displayed in such a way that someone can admire it (i.e., you!) every day.

* As for the first list, destroy it by whatever means are most pleasurable. You've officially fired your critic. Maybe you should say it out loud—YOU'RE FIRED!—just in case that critic of yours is hard of hearing.

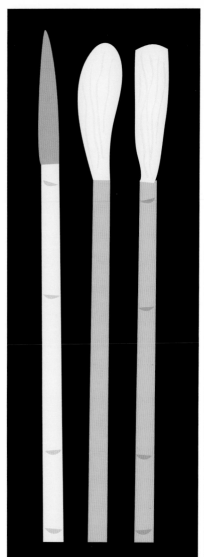

Zen artists take a spontaneous and free-flowing approach to Japanese ink painting, or Sumi-e. *Creating the likeness of an object is secondary to capturing its essence, and while technique is important, the priority is expression. Using simple materials and basic ideas, the painter lets go of ego and self to become one with the brush, the paint, the paper, and the subject. If you want to try your hand at Zen painting, here's how to start.*

Simple Strokes

* Traditionally, Japanese artists work on the floor, kneeling over their work. If you're comfortable painting in this fashion, give it a shot (you might want to put a pillow under your knees). If not, sit at a desk or table.

* Take a few moments to clear your head. Breathe deeply, relax, and bring yourself into the present.

* Place the felt pad on the table or floor and your paper on top of the pad. Painting on an absorbent surface will help collect any water that soaks through the paper, keeping the painting free of puddles.

* Arrange your tools in front of you, making sure your work space is organized and tidy. Be deliberate and purposeful in your actions. Preparation is as much a part of the experience as the painting itself is.

continued >

What You'll Need

Felt pad

Rice paper

Water dish

Ink stone

Sumi-e ink stick

Brushes

Damp rag

Plate

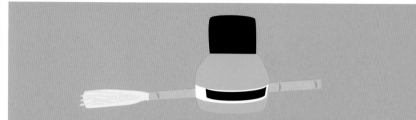

* Fill up your water dish. Place a few drops of water on the flat section of the ink stone. Rub the ink stick in circular motions against the wet stone surface until it produces a liquid. Don't rush this process. Make sure the ink is well ground and isn't pasty. Allow the liquid ink to run into the recessed well of the stone. (You may need to help it along with the stick.)

* Wet your brush with water and wipe the excess water on the damp rag.

* Dip the tip of the brush in the ink, loading only the first third of the bristles. Run the brush over the plate to spread the ink to the rest of the bristles.

* Hold the brush between your thumb and first finger, allowing the handle to rest on your middle finger. Begin to paint in continuous strokes. Try not to stop and start; your movements should flow one into another. Keep your hand and body relaxed. Breathe naturally.

* Play with a variety of strokes. Get comfortable with the brush and the paint.

* When you feel ready, draw a tree or flower, maybe a circle or square, whatever strikes you, but keep it simple. Try to maintain some sort of momentum and don't spend time on details. Use simple, fluid lines.

* As you complete each painting, set it aside to dry.

The haiku is a unique Japanese literary tradition taking much of its breath from the world of Zen. It is a seventeen-syllable poem composed of three lines of five, seven, and five syllables, in that order. The spirit of a haiku is grounded in the awareness of the present and the ability to see the extraordinary in the ordinary. Despite its simplicity, the haiku is a powerful means of expressing the often overlooked beauty and significance of the day-to-day. Take a moment to discover the miraculous goings-on around you, and craft that discovery into a haiku of your very own.

High Art

* Take a deep breath.

* Spend a few minutes soaking everything in.
  Observe yourself. Observe your surroundings.
  What do you see, hear, smell, feel?

* Close your eyes. What comes to mind?
  An image? A word? A color?
  Whatever it is, run with it.
  Paint a vivid picture in simple words.

Haikus are brief, bold.
Turn a moment into words,
Discover beauty.

As with the other Zen arts, you could say that the art of flower arrangement is actually more about the arranging than the arrangement. Contemplative yet spontaneous, the gentle handling of the flowers becomes a vehicle through which you can meditate on their beauty, life's beauty, and your own inner beauty.

Zen and the Art of Flower Arrangement

What You'll Need

A *kubari*, or Y-shaped branch (you can cut this from a larger, bendable branch)

Vase

Pruning shears

3 pliable branches of flowers (take these from your yard or pick them up at your local florist)

Water

* Use a few minutes to calm your mind and body. Take a deep breath and focus on the present moment.

* Arrange your materials. Notice details. How do the flowers smell? What is their color and texture?

* Put the Y-shaped branch in the vase first. Insert it horizontally—it will serve as support for the other flowers. Push it down about one to two inches into the vase and make sure it fits properly and is securely in place. If you need to adjust its size for a better fit, do so now.

* The arrangement is guided by the Zen principle of three, the three separate flower branches symbolizing the three points of the universe: heaven, earth, and humanity. Gently place the longest flower branch in the vase, followed by the remaining two branches. Arrange the branches so that they appear to be one branch growing in the shape of a triangle. You may need to trim the branches to get the correct effect.

* Add water, set out the vase, and enjoy.

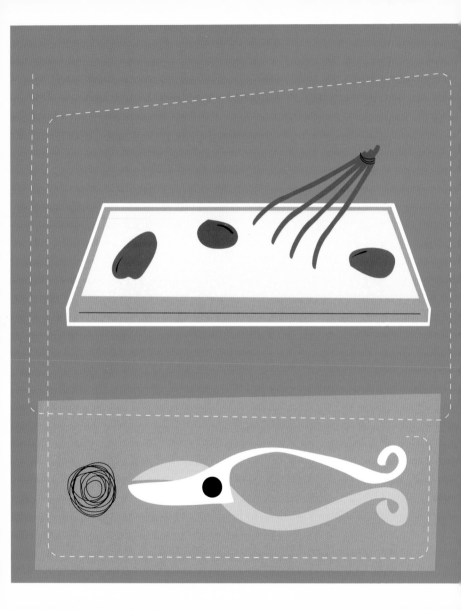

A Zen rock garden is a unique and beautiful spot for meditation and reflection. Stark and simple, its sand-and-stone setting is ideal for clearing a cluttered head and bringing mind and body together. You can capture the spirit of a traditional garden by creating a miniature version. (No pruning or watering necessary!) Here's how to cultivate your very own. Keep your miniature rock garden near your desk, and you will always have a calm, peaceful place to meditate within reach.

Rock Gardening

* First you are going to create a small rake using the four twigs and thread. Hold the twigs together at one end. Wrap the thread around that end, securing it with a knot. Cut off any excess thread. Flatten out the twigs so they take the shape of a rake.

* Pour the sand into the box top.

* Slowly shake the box top from side to side until the sand has a flat, even surface. Set the box down on a tabletop or counter.

* Contemplate the garden, and imagine yourself walking into it. You are surrounded by peace and serenity. Using the rake, create a design in the sand—straight lines, concentric circles, whatever suits your mood.

* Incorporate the stones into your design. One by one, gently place each stone in the sand. Notice the relationship between form and space.

* Enjoy a few moments of calm and quiet in your garden.

What You'll Need

4 small twigs approximately 3 inches in length

Heavy-duty household thread

Scissors

2 tablespoons of sand

Small box top (roughly 4 inches by 3 inches)

3 small stones

Singing is liberating, invigorating, and downright fun. Belting out tunes not only gives you an outlet for pent-up emotions and energy, but it also invigorates your soul. Next time you need a release, turn up the volume and let it rip.

Finding Your Voice

* This is an exercise you'll probably want to do solo (or with a very, very good, tone-deaf friend), so find a secluded spot where you won't disturb anyone.

* Warm up a bit. Shake out your arms, do a few neck rolls, maybe run through a scale or two. When you're feeling ready to rock, turn on your favorite song and grab a microphone. (A candle, mixing spoon, flashlight, banana, ruler, or small water bottle will do.)

* Picture yourself on stage in front of thousands of adoring fans. Now sing your heart out for them. Give all of yourself to the song. Scream and jump and spin around. You are a rock star.

* Don't worry about your singing abilities; frankly, most of us won't sound good. No big deal. Instead, turn your focus to the act of singing, not the sound of your voice.

* Pay attention to your mind and body and how they respond. Is your heart beating naturally or has it sped up? What emotions are surfacing?

* If you start to feel overwhelmed by emotions (and this may happen—you're really stirring things up inside), let them out. Scream, cry, laugh—whatever feels good.

Glow-How

The car provides the perfect venue for an intimate concert. Next time you're stuck in traffic or in the midst of a hellish commute, instead of screaming at the car in front of you, use that energy to sing!

A big part of meditation is getting reacquainted with yourself and all of the qualities and curiosities that make you you. *What's amazing is that the more we get to know ourselves, the more we realize just how much there is to learn. When we let go of scattered thoughts and unnecessary emotions, we make room for more important stuff, and interests and ideas we never knew existed can start to surface.*

Go On, Try It!

* Grab a pen and paper.

* Take twenty minutes and write down everything you've ever (secretly or openly) wanted to try. Perhaps your itch is to take an African dance class, or maybe you've always wanted to indulge in a weekend writing workshop, or could it be that you simply long to wear cherry-red lipstick? Whatever the inkling might be, write it down.

* Keep the list close by, where you will see it frequently.

* Start working your way down the list. Sign up for that pottery class or photography clinic. And one by one turn those budding interests into full-fledged passions.

* As you take on each challenge, practice the Be the Ball exercise on page 61. Every new activity provides another opportunity to incorporate meditation into your life.

CHAPTER FOUR

Freestyle Meditations

Meditation is about coming alive, experiencing life, and being your true, unadulterated self. Sometimes it's hard to grasp the underlying intention of meditation through the traditional means. For some people the techniques can feel awkward. That's okay. There are countless ways to meditate. In fact, you don't even have to call it meditating; you can call it living! Turn anything you do into a simple meditation by including just one extra criterion: your honest attention.

In this chapter you'll see how easy it is to incorporate meditation into your daily life. Try the cooking exercise or the laughing meditation, take a silent lunch or have a tea party. You'll soon see that meditating isn't so unnatural after all.

Reading your favorite magazine or grooving to your newest CD can also serve as a therapeutic form of meditation. It is time spent relaxing and reengaging with yourself, the very point of meditation. The trick is to find the time—or, rather, to make the time. Like any other meditation technique, this too will take practice and discipline.

Lessons in Leisure

* Pull out your calendar. Pick one night this week and pencil this in: MY TIME. MY TIME means no visitors, no phone calls, and absolutely no laundry or housecleaning!

* Put a DO NOT DISTURB sign on your door.

* Unplug the phones and any other means to outside contact.

* Draw a bath, pull out your dusty guitar, flip through a magazine, do whatever calms you down, helps you relax, and makes you happy.

* Savor every moment.

In some sects of Hinduism, people practice a twilight meditation at dusk and dawn known as the sandhya. *Below is an adaptation that can be a simple yet invigorating addition to your morning ritual.*

Sunrise Sandhyas

* Get up fifteen minutes before you normally would.

* Take a warm shower, brush your teeth, and have a glass of water.

* Clear your mind and body with a breathing exercise. Breath in for four counts and out for four counts. Do this for one minute.

* Recite a favorite poem, quote, or song. (The Hindus usually read from ancient scriptures, but speaking the words of a favorite poet or musician will also work just fine.)

* Offer thanks to yourself and to all human beings.

* Do a five-minute meditation using a focal point of your choice. The Hindus often use the symbol of Ganesh, the elephant god who represents the ability to transcend any obstacles or barriers on the road to wisdom. For kicks, before your next *sandhya,* pick up a Ganesh statuette or something that will represent the idea of Ganesh, like a small elephant figurine. It may make the practice a little more authentic and meaningful to you.

* Start your day energized, refreshed, and focused.

If you're not quite ready for a sunrise meditation, you can still do yourself a huge service by getting up thirty minutes early. This might sound like a wild concept, especially to you night owls, but it's definitely worth a try. The extra time provides the opportunity to get your body, mind, and soul balanced and in order before your day begins. Rushing creates unnecessary stress, anxiety, and panic that can linger into the afternoon. Gather your composure before you walk out the door and spend the rest of the day thanking yourself.

Snooze-Free Zone

* Set your alarm for thirty minutes earlier than you normally do.

* When it goes off, get up—no hitting the snooze button!

* Do a gentle forward bend to stretch your back and hamstrings. Shake out your arms and legs.

* Hit the shower. Linger a little and don't rush the bathing ritual or the morning ablutions.

* Eat a light breakfast.

* Spend a few minutes relaxing. Read the paper, stare out the window, do a few yoga postures— whatever feels good to you.

* Take five minutes to write up your to-do list and organize yourself for the day.

* Walk out the door calm, cool, and collected.

Glow-How

Try this new "early thing" throughout the day. Start showing up for meetings, lunch dates, and appointments just a tad ahead of time. That way you allow yourself a few minutes to get organized, breathe, and relax.

Nothing feels better than a good hug. No, not the standard quick squeeze and pat on the back, but a real, sustained, wholehearted embrace. The kind of hug you feel in your soul, the kind of hug that makes your whole body smile.
Here's a variation of the hug to try on friends and family.

Hug Someone

* Make hugging and hugging often a general practice. Your mom, best friend, or roommate (even though she left dirty dishes in the sink) are all good candidates. It's one of the nicest things you can do for yourself and for others.

* When you hug, hug like you mean it. Be aware of your connection with the person you're hugging. Don't get distracted or let your mind wander. Take a deep breath, relax your body, calm your mind, and really feel the person in your arms.

Glow-How

Okay, so not everyone wants to be hugged all the time. Use the same principles when shaking hands or greeting someone. Holding hands is another great way to share a meditative moment with someone you love!

Like other forms of meditation, laughter is a great way to clear the mind and heal the soul. It's also a powerful stress reliever, energizer, and general mood enhancer; plus, it just feels good. Initially this exercise may seem strained and unnatural, but give it a try. As you continue to laugh, the positive energy will soon take over, as will the bona fide belly laughter. Here's how to get your giggle going.

Belly Laugh

* Try this alone or with friends.

* Begin with some simple stretches—roll your head, do a forward and backward bend, twist left, twist right, shake out your arms and legs.

* Now, laugh! Make a funny face, touch your tongue to your nose, repeat a silly word aloud until it sounds really silly—whatever makes you crack a smile. Let the laughter course through your entire body.

* Laugh until your cheeks hurt or you fall over, whatever comes first.

* Sit in silence for a moment. Enjoy the positive vibes running through your body. Relax, breathe, and smile.

Stop the racket! Noise—internal and external chatter, car horns, radios, televisions—pumps through our bodies every day, robbing us of the natural peace and serenity that comes with silence. Unfortunately, silence is hard to come by these days, so it's important that we seek it out. Taking a silent lunch is an easy way to fit some quiet time into your schedule and will allow you a few stolen moments to turn down the volume.

Silent Lunch

* Grab a bagged lunch.

* Head to a place where you know there is at least relative silence. Try a park or an abandoned meeting room or classroom. Your office will also work—just make sure to turn off the phone and shut the door.

* Have a seat and enjoy your silent lunch. Clear your head of its babble, don't talk to anyone, and if someone talks to you or asks to join you, kindly let them know you're taking some much-needed private time. They will certainly understand.

The Way of Tea is a centuries-old form of meditation owing much of its character to the Zen philosophies. You'll find that the beauty of this ceremony lies not in its pomp but in its simplicity.

Tea Party

* Find a quiet spot (with a heat source within close proximity). Your living room is fine, an outside garden even better.

* Heat the water and set out your tea set. Clear your thoughts and focus on the ceremony.

* Scoop out the tea, present the leaves to your guests, then drop the leaves in the teapot.

* Pour some hot water into the teapot and then quickly pour it out. (You're cleaning off the leaves. According to the custom, this liquid is unfit to drink.)

* Promptly pour fresh hot water into the pot. Allow the tea to steep for a few moments.

* The cups should be arranged in a line. In a continuous stream, pour the tea into the cups, from one end to the other, moving back and forth until the cups are filled.

* Offer the tea by sweeping your hand across the cups.

* Enjoy the presence of your friends, and the peace and harmony of a simple sip of tea.

What You'll Need
———
Heat source

Teakettle

Water

Teapot

Cups

Tea

A few friends

Calling all commuters: This exercise is for you. A car ride is the perfect time for a little mindful meditation. Peaceful, private, the car can become your personal sanctuary. The keys to a successful drive-time meditation are simple, good tunes, an open and alert mind, and an appreciation of the journey. Use of the horn is strictly prohibited, as is the lead foot. (The finger, also off-limits.) This time is meant to bring you peace and tranquility, not anger and aggression.

Ride It Out

* Start the car, put on some soft, mellow music, take a deep breath, and cruise. Get comfortable in your seat. Keep your back straight and your shoulders relaxed.

* Slow down! No racing from point A to point B, no weaving or tailgating—just drive. Don't think about yesterday or tomorrow. Think about your driving. Drive safely and attentively, aware of your surroundings and the journey you are taking.

* When someone cuts you off, just take a deep breath and, on the exhalation, smile at life.

Glow-How

As a passenger, your car-ride meditations can go deeper. Turn to the window and really take in the view. Spend some time focusing on your breath, and let your worries drop away with each passing mile.

Using the ancient Chinese art of feng shui, enhance your automotive chi *(energy) for a more harmonious ride. Here are a few suggestions on how to get your car's energy moving.*

Cures for Your Car

* Clean it out. A messy car can block your energy flow, while a tidy car will provide fresh, clean energy. Ditch whatever you don't need.

* Hit the service station. Improve your car's energy value by making sure it's running efficiently. Anything in disrepair will block energy flow, so even after it's gotten the thumbs-up from the mechanic, remember to check your oil and tire pressure on a regular basis.

* Add some life to the car. Fresh flowers bring vitality and energy to any environment. Use your car's cup holder as a spot for some flora.

* Stimulate your energy and awareness with pleasant and uplifting odors. Burn some incense or a fragrant car candle.

* Make sure you've always got some good tunes on hand. Good music cultivates positive vibes.

The kitchen is a perfect sanctuary for meditation, a quiet, solitary place to lose yourself in the process of chopping, blending, and seasoning. You'll need just one additional ingredient: mindfulness.

Culinary Escapes

* Pick a night this week and get ready to prepare yourself a feast infused with awareness.

* Turn on some soulful music and light a candle.

* Carefully set out all of your ingredients. Keep your space clean and organized. A chaotic kitchen will wreak havoc on a calm mind.

* Slowly, consciously begin cooking. Take your time and enjoy each step as you mince, mix, and sauté. Flow from one step into the next.

* When your dinner is ready, sit down and really enjoy your food. Eat slowly and savor each delicious bite.

According to Zen Buddhists, true enlightenment comes when a person realizes her intimate connection to nature and embraces a feeling of oneness with the universe. For many, this is the ultimate goal of meditation. It's very tough to achieve, but some folks have actually done it, so there is hope for you! (Besides, the path to enlightenment is just as important as getting there.) Working in a garden is a perfect way to start your journey to nirvana—it puts you in touch with the earth and brings you closer to nature. If you don't have a yard, not to worry—it's easy to create an indoor garden. All you need is a window box or large container, indoor plants, and some dirt. (The staff at your local nursery should be able to help you find suitable flora and soil for your climate and space.)

Garden Guru

* Put on some grubby clothes, dust off those garden tools, and head outside.

* If you've never gardened before, don't fret; this is the perfect opportunity for you to learn something new. Take it slow and easy. The idea is to relax and enjoy.

* Stand at the edge of your yard. Take a few deep breaths, pull yourself into the present, and survey the scene. Is there any area that's crying out for your attention? Start there.

continued >

Glow-How

To start your garden, you'll need some basic supplies. Get your hands on a pair of garden shears, a small spade, a hand pruner, a long-handled pruner, and round-headed shovel, and you will be ready to go. Make sure you have a leaf rake, a broom, and a large bag for easy clean-up. Protect yourself with gardening gloves and a cute straw hat, and don't forget the bug repellent and sunscreen.

* Decide what you want to do and create a plan of attack. Remember, meditation is about focus, so do one thing at a time. Weed, plow, and then sow.

* Clear your head of extraneous thoughts and concentrate on the task at hand. What texture is the dirt? What color are the flowers? Do they have a scent? Then move the focus to yourself. How does the earth feel in your hands? Rough? Moist? Cold? Does the scent of the flowers please you? What other forms of life do you see in the garden? Do they notice you?

* Feel yourself become part of the garden.

Listening may seem automatic: Someone speaks, you listen. But a lot of us hear words without really considering their meaning. The next time you're having lunch or coffee with a friend, try this fine-tuning exercise. You may discover that listening is more of an acquired skill than a natural reflex.

Tuning In

* Take a deep breath, clear your head, settle in, and really listen. Focus on your companion's words as they are expressed. Thoughtfully, attentively hear what he or she is saying.

* Don't let your eyes glaze over as your attention starts to fade into yesterday or tomorrow. Listen.

* Notice your own body language and your own instinctual desire to jump in and speak. Notice the amount of difficulty you may or may not be having staying engaged in the conversation.

Glow-How

For a real test of your listening skills, try this exercise at a party. Free-flowing cocktails, fancy dresses, and eye-catching appetizers will most certainly test your focus and concentration.

A massage is a great way to put your mind and body back in touch. It not only helps to relieve stress and tension, it makes you aware of the areas of your body that perhaps you've neglected or, worse, forgotten about altogether. Getting a professional massage is, of course, the best option, but if that seems unlikely or beyond your budget, you can always give yourself one. Here's how.

Give Yourself a Hand

* Let your chin fall to your chest and relax your shoulders.

* Rub your palms together vigorously to warm them up.

* With your right hand, knead and squeeze with your fingers and palm from the top of your neck, down your left trapezius muscle, into your shoulder, down your arm, and into your hand. Yes, your hands need massaging, too! Now reverse the direction.

* Repeat on the right side with your left hand.

Make your morning shower a special meditation time. Instead of your habitual quick rinse, slow it down, clear your head, and spend a few minutes savoring the time alone. (It may be all you get today.) In the tradition of the Japanese public baths, add a cold plunge to the end of your morning ritual. The cold water will stimulate your circulatory system, close your pores, and wake you up.

Japanese Shower

* Ease into the shower. Don't think about the day to come; just be aware of yourself and your breath.

* Stand under the water for a few minutes. Feel your mind and body slowly start to come alive. Breathe consciously and rhythmically.

* Focus on yourself and what you're doing. Take in the scent of your soap or shampoo. Feel the texture of your loofah or washcloth against your skin.

* Once you've finished washing, gradually change the water temperature from hot to warm to cold. Revel in the cool water for a moment or two. Feel your mind, body, and soul come alive.

Bath-Time Essentials

Mineral bath salts

Exfoliating body scrub and/or loofah

Pumice stone

Body wash

Body lotion

Face cream

Bottled water

Tea

Soft music

Glow-How

Bathing can be a sacred ritual, and the bath, your personal sanctuary. Add a soak in the tub to your weekly routine and feel the difference in mind, body, and soul.

Spend an hour or two this afternoon applying the principles of meditation to your everyday life. No, don't run back to your meditation cushion; this is meant to be a hands-on experience. You need to be out in the field. The idea is to learn how to bring your calm and aware mind, relaxed body, good posture, and strong presence into your day-to-day life.

Practical Experience

* When you walk, be aware of each step.

* When you sit, sit with your spine straight and your shoulders relaxed.

* When you breathe, breathe deeply and deliberately.

* When you communicate, speak thoughtfully and listen attentively.

* When you work or study, focus entirely on the project at hand.

Digging Deeper

Bennett-Goleman, Tara. *Emotional Alchemy: How the Mind Can Heal the Heart.* New York: Harmony Books, 2001.

Cameron, Julia. *The Artist's Way: A Spiritual Path to Higher Creativity.* New York: Jeremy P. Tarcher/Putnam, 1992.

Dalai Lama of Tibet. *Awakening the Mind, Lightening the Heart.* San Francisco: HarperSanFrancisco, 1995.

Hewitt, James. *The Complete Yoga Book: Yoga of Breathing, Yoga of Posture, and Yoga of Meditation.* New York: Schocken Books Inc., 1977.

Moore, Dinty W. *The Accidental Buddhist: Mindfulness, Enlightenment, and Still Sitting.* Chapel Hill: Algonquin Books of Chapel Hill, 1997.

Nhat Hanh, Thich. *Peace Is Every Step: The Path of Mindfulness in Everyday Life.* New York: Bantam Books, 1991.

———. *The Blooming of a Lotus: Guided Meditation Exercises for Healing and Transformation.* Boston: Beacon Press, 1993.

Rinpoche, Sogyal. *The Tibetan Book of Living and Dying.* San Francisco: HarperSanFrancisco, 1994.

Salzberg, Sharon. *Lovingkindness: The Revolutionary Art of Happiness.* Boston: Shambhala Publications, Inc., 1995.

Suzuki, Shunryu. *Zen Mind, Beginner's Mind.* New York: Weatherhill, 1997.